Contents

D0124388

Introduction

Like a child and its mother, the face of Maryland reflects the beauty of the United States. Although it is a small state, Maryland contains a sampling of what is found throughout the nation. Forested mountain ridges line the landscape in western Maryland. Fields and orchards spread out across valleys between the peaks. Eastern Maryland is dominated by the Chesapeake Bay, with its small fishing towns and big city ports. Older cities, such as St. Mary's City, Annapolis, and Baltimore, hold the memory of our country's struggle for freedom. The best of our nation belongs to Maryland.

The Baltimore Orioles play baseball in Oriole Park at Camden Yards. The park, which opened in 1992, reflects Maryland's love for the sport.

STECK-VAUGHN

PORTRAIT OF AMERICA

Maryland

Kathleen Thompson

A Turner Book

RSVP

RAINTREE
STECK-VAUGHN
PUBLISHERS

The Steck-Vaughn Company

Austin, Texas

Maryland

Chesapeake Bay, tobacco, Annapolis

The Land of Tolerance

Over ten thousand years ago, prehistoric Native American hunters roamed the land we now call Maryland. Over the centuries, they began to split into many different groups. Most of these groups set up permanent villages by A.D. 1000.

Almost all of these Native American groups spoke variations of a language called Algonquian. Algonquian-speaking groups in the Maryland area included the Nanticoke, Piscataway, Patuxent, and Yaocomaco people. At that time most of them lived in huts built from branches and covered with bark or grass. They hunted, fished, and grew beans, corn, and squash. Many of them also harvested oysters and other shellfish from the Chesapeake Bay. They left huge piles of empty shells, some of which still exist.

On the very northern border of present-day Maryland lived the Susquehannock. The lifestyle of the Susquehannock was similar to that of their Algonquin neighbors. They were more aggressive, though, and they sometimes attacked the Algonquins.

The New England colonies began to produce bricks in the 1700s, making it possible to build houses like this one. This house was designed to look like an English country house.

The first European to explore the Chesapeake Bay region of Maryland thoroughly was John Smith of Virginia. Smith arrived from the English settlement in Jamestown, Virginia. He mapped out the region and reported back that it would be a good place for a new settlement. Traders soon traveled north from Virginia to exchange items, such as tools and cloth for furs, with the Native Americans. In 1631 William Claiborne, Virginia's secretary of state, set up a trading post on Kent Island, located on the eastern shore of the Chesapeake Bay.

At the same time that the Virginia colonists were settling down in the Chesapeake Bay area, an English official named Sir George Calvert chose the same area for a new settlement. Unaware that Claiborne was already settling there, Calvert, lord of the English province of Baltimore, asked King Charles I to grant him the land. The king agreed, but Sir George died before his promise was officially fulfilled. In 1632 the king gave the land to Sir George's son Cecilius.

The Calvert family was Roman Catholic. They had often been persecuted in England for their religion. Cecilius was determined to start a colony based on the acceptance of all Christian religions. Late in 1633 Cecilius sent his younger brother, Leonard, to establish this colony. Leonard set out from England with two ships, the *Ark* and the *Dove*, and about 150 colonists of different religions. They reached St. Clements Island, in the southern part of present-day Maryland, on March 25, 1634. Two days later they settled near a small inlet on the western side of

Sir George Calvert, founder of Maryland, died before the Maryland charter was granted. Calvert originally tried to settle in Virginia but was not allowed to due to his religious beliefs.

Chesapeake Bay. They called their new settlement St. Marys, known today as St. Mary's City. The Calverts named their new colony Maryland, in honor of the king's wife, Queen Henrietta Maria.

The Maryland settlers cultivated wheat, corn, and tobacco. Tobacco was the most profitable of these crops. Farmers set up tobacco plantations, or large farming communities run by a single landowner. As these plantations grew, more people were needed to farm them, and plantation owners began importing African slaves for this work.

Maryland's plantations and farms were spreading into Native American territory. A number of Native American groups fought to keep the settlers off their land. They attacked many of the settlements, but they were overcome by the heavily armed colonists. In addition, many Native Americans caught deadly diseases such as smallpox. So many Native Americans were killed or died of these diseases that the Susquehannock were forced to stop their raids. The Susquehannock turned over their land to the colonists in 1652. They were the last of the warring Native American groups in the area.

Maryland's colonial population grew rapidly. This growth sparked a border dispute with Maryland's northern neighbor, Pennsylvania. Lord Baltimore and William Penn, the proprietor of Pennsylvania, agreed to call in surveyors to settle the border dispute for good. Charles Mason and Jeremiah Dixon finished measuring the border in 1767. The Mason-Dixon Line not only separated Maryland from Pennsylvania, but it also marked the boundary between the North and South.

As the colonies continued to prosper, Great Britain sought a share of their profits. The British Parliament placed high taxes on many goods that the colonists imported from Great Britain. Most colonists saw these taxes as unfair. Groups were assembled to discuss breaking away from British rule and uniting the colonies into a single nation. The Revolutionary War soon followed, beginning in Massachusetts in April 1775. Maryland delegates cast their ballots for independence at the second Continental Congress held in July 1776.

No Revolutionary War battles were fought in Maryland, but the state showed its patriotism by sending 23,000 soldiers to fight the British. George

Mid-1700s farming methods are re-created at the National Colonial Farm Museum in Accokeek.

Washington recognized the bravery of the Maryland volunteers. He called them "troops of the line," giving the state its nickname, the "Old Line State."

The Revolutionary War officially ended in Annapolis, Maryland, when the Treaty of Paris was signed at the Maryland State House there on January 14, 1784. Four years later Maryland approved the Constitution of the United States and became the seventh state in the new Union.

In 1791 Maryland and Virginia donated portions of their territories to form the nation's capital, the District of Columbia. Maryland continued to prosper. Baltimore, by then Maryland's major port, also became a major American city. It was the largest city south of the Mason-Dixon Line.

The new nation's struggles with Great Britain were not yet over, however. Trade between the United States and other countries was thriving. This meant that the United States was in competition with Great Britain, which was a leader in international trade. The British began harassing American trade ships, and when they refused to stop, President James Madison asked Congress to declare war. The War of 1812 had begun.

Maryland hadn't played a very important role in the Revolutionary War. But now the thriving port of Baltimore looked valuable to the British. In August 1814, the British tested American strength by attacking the nation's capital. They set fire to a number of buildings in Washington, D.C., including the White House. One month later the British moved on to attack Baltimore's Fort McHenry.

The Capitol is located in Washington, D.C., which is adjacent to Maryland.

It was the Battle of Baltimore that inspired Francis Scott Key to write "The Star-Spangled Banner." Key was a Baltimore native who had been captured by the British. He was held prisoner on a British ship in Baltimore Harbor. From there he watched the attack on Fort McHenry. When the smoke cleared after the bombardment, Fort McHenry's American flag was still flying. The sight of the flag inspired Key to write the verses that have become our national anthem.

The United States and Great Britain signed a treaty that ended the war in December 1814. At last the United States could turn back to the task of building a new nation. One of the first projects that Maryland undertook was to build a national road called the National Pike. This road was also called the Cumberland Road. In 1818 it connected Cumberland in western Maryland to Wheeling, Virginia. By 1840 it stretched eight hundred miles to Illinois. It was the first national road in the United States.

Maryland also played an important role in linking the states by railroad. Construction of the Baltimore &

The battle at Fort McHenry was the inspiration for "The Star-Spangled Banner." The song was officially adopted as the national anthem by Congress in 1931.

Ohio Railroad was started in 1828. The Baltimore & Ohio was the first steam-powered passenger train line in the United States. Baltimore was now thriving in trade both overseas and across the nation.

In 1861 Maryland's progress was interrupted by war once again. This time the war was between the states. Arguments between the Northern and Southern states had grown steadily louder in the past twenty years, mostly over slavery. Maryland was soon caught in the middle of these arguments, in terms of both its geography and its ideas.

Slavery in the North was slowly being abolished. The abolitionist, or antislavery, movement

Fort Washington in Prince George's County was built in 1809 and first used in the Civil War. The fort is now a military base and part of a nearly 350-acre national park.

began to pressure the Southern states to outlaw slavery. Maryland had more free African Americans than any other state by 1850. Even so, many of the state's tobacco planters still depended on slaves to run their plantations. Many other people in Maryland thought slavery was wrong, however. When the Civil War broke out in April 1861, Maryland soldiers fought on both sides. Although Maryland was south of the Mason-Dixon line, the state remained in the Union.

One of the most devastating battles of the Civil War took place in western Maryland near Sharpsburg. In 1862, Union forces met the Confederates at the Battle of Antietam, at Antietam Creek. In a single day, more than 23,000 soldiers were killed or wounded.

The Confederacy surrendered on April 9, 1865. Many people on both sides rejoiced at the end of the bloodshed. Five days later, John Wilkes Booth, a Maryland actor, shot and killed President Abraham

Harriet Tubman (far left) was born a slave in Maryland. She helped found the Underground Railroad, an organization that helped more than three hundred slaves escape to freedom.

Lincoln in Washington, D.C. Booth was angry at Lincoln for the outcome of the war. People across the country mourned Lincoln's death.

This photo shows some of the war dead of the Battle of Antietam. September 17, 1862, was one of the bloodiest days of the Civil War.

Following the war, business and industry boomed, especially in Baltimore. The city's population grew rapidly between 1865 and 1900. Two of Baltimore's most successful citizens made contributions that the city benefits from today. Enoch Pratt, who made his money from the iron industry, donated over eight hundred thousand dollars to build the Enoch Pratt Free Library in 1882. Johns Hopkins, who owned most of the Baltimore & Ohio Railroad, donated seven million dollars to build a university and a medical school. Both schools were completed by 1889. Johns Hopkins University and its medical school are among the most highly respected schools in the country.

When the United States entered World War I in 1917, Maryland sent more than sixty thousand soldiers to fight. Others who didn't go overseas helped out at home. Maryland's shipyards expanded to meet wartime needs. So did the state's factories, especially the food-canning industry.

After the war, Maryland prospered until the early 1930s when the Great Depression fell upon the nation. More than 13 million people across the nation were out of work. The country's economy was in ruins. Over

The Peabody Library at Johns Hopkins University contains many documents concerning medical history.

The 4.35-mile Chesapeake Bay Bridge was opened in 1952. A parallel bridge was added in 1980 because traffic had gotten so heavy.

The National Aquarium is part of Baltimore's Inner Harbor. The Inner Harbor was developed to attract visitors to Baltimore.

half of Maryland's factories closed during the Depression. Production didn't pick up again until the United States entered World War II in 1941. Maryland's factories increased their output to help win the war, just as they had done for World War I. Once again Maryland sent many of its citizens to fight. This time over 250,000 men and women answered the call.

One major development in the state during World War II was the opening of Camp David in 1942. Camp David is the retreat home of the President of the United States. This two-hundred-acre compound in northern Maryland's Catoctin Mountain Park was first visited by President Franklin D. Roosevelt. Maryland is proud that every President since then has spent time relaxing in its peaceful mountains.

One of Maryland's—and the nation's—main social concerns after World War II was the fight for civil rights. The term *civil rights* refers to equal opportunity for people of all races. Schools were among the institutions that did not provide equal opportunity. In 1954 the United States Supreme Court ruled that all schools must be opened to all students regardless of their race. Maryland carried out this ruling more rapidly than any other southern state.

Maryland citizens of all races fought for civil rights outside the classroom, too. In 1954 African Americans were voted into the state legislature for the first time since the late 1800s. In 1967 Maryland became the first southern state to pass equal housing laws. These laws helped people who had not been allowed to live in certain neighborhoods or buildings because of their race.

Beginning in the 1950s, conditions began to worsen in Maryland's cities, especially Baltimore. More people moved out of the cities and into newer communities in the surrounding areas. These areas, called suburbs, sprang up very quickly throughout the United States. Cities were hurt economically because many of those people who moved away earned the highest incomes. To raise money for its financially troubled cities, Maryland instituted a state lottery in 1972.

The state soon raised enough money for a major renovation of Baltimore. The city opened Harborplace, an elaborate shopping and restaurant complex, in 1980. An aquarium and a marina also were opened in the area. Tourists and new businesses soon arrived. Many cities across the nation followed Baltimore's example of successful city renovation. Renovations of other areas of Baltimore continue. Plans include building a new marine technology center, two condominium communities, and expanding the Baltimore Convention Center.

Many people have called Maryland "America in Miniature," because this small state displays so many characteristics of the United States as a whole. This nickname applies to Maryland's history, too, which has played such an important part in the country's history from the very beginning.

Almost 150 shops and restaurants draw tourists to Baltimore's Harborplace, completed in 1980.

Mr. Civil Rights

Thurgood Marshall learned something as a schoolboy that very few other students have had the opportunity to learn. What he learned made him not only a success as a man but also as one of the most highly respected judges in our country's history. Unfortunately, it all came about as a result of his being a troublemaker in school!

As a child growing up in West Baltimore, Thurgood Marshall was often punished for speaking out of turn. The school principal sent him to the basement on these occasions and did not allow him back to class until he had learned a passage from the United States Constitution. By the time Marshall graduated, he knew the whole Constitution by heart!

There were a few things about the Constitution that Marshall found confusing, though. A section of

Before he was appointed to the Supreme Court, Thurgood Marshall (far left) won 29 of the 32 cases he argued before the Court.

In July 1963, police arrested 223 demonstrators and dragged them to a bus to be taken to jail. The demonstrators were protesting segregation at a Baltimore amusement park.

the document, the Fourteenth Amendment, promised equal rights for everyone. As an African American living in the early 1900s, Thurgood Marshall knew that not everyone had equal rights in spite of the Constitution's guarantee. He was keenly aware that state segregation laws separated African Americans from others in society. He knew that African Americans were not allowed to compete for the best jobs or go to the same schools that others went to. In many places, African Americans were not even allowed to drink from the same drinking fountains as others.

21

Linda Brown was nine years old when her father sued the Topeka, Kansas, Board of Education.

As he learned more about the Constitution, Marshall realized he wanted to do something to carry out the laws of the country. When he was old enough, he attended law school at Howard University. This school had been established two years after the Civil War for the purpose of educating former slaves. While at Howard University, Thurgood Marshall was taught by two teachers who had a lasting influence on his life. Their names were William Henry Hastie and Charles Hamilton Houston. Hastie later became the country's first African American judge appointed to the United States Circuit Court of Appeals. Houston was a lawyer who was very important in the early civil rights movement. Hastie and Houston reminded Marshall that, according to the Constitution, civil rights are personal rights that every person has. They taught him that he could do something about the way African Americans were treated by society. They also challenged him to question laws that allowed segregation.

In 1933 Thurgood Marshall graduated at the top of his class. He soon opened his own law office. No one wanted his services during that first year; he didn't have a single customer. But slowly clients did come. And most were glad they did. Marshall was smart, and he knew the law well. He was also a fine speaker. Word of his skills as a lawyer began to spread. He didn't make much money at first. Most of his clients were poor and couldn't afford to pay him. Instead of money, however, he earned respect.

In 1934 the National Association for the Advancement of Colored People (NAACP) asked Thurgood Marshall to be the group's lawyer. The NAACP is an organization that had been established to end racial discrimination. The job paid nothing, but Marshall was used to that. He felt proud to be part of a group fighting for the civil rights of African Americans. In the years that followed, Marshall battled segregation in the schools—and anywhere else he found it. He wanted everyone to know that segregation was wrong. The newspapers called him "Mr. Civil Rights."

In 1953 Thurgood Marshall argued the most important case of his career. It was known as *Brown* v. *Board of Education of Topeka, Kansas.* The problem was a familiar one. Linda Brown and other African American children in Topeka, Kansas, had not been allowed to go to public schools with other children. The schools were segregated. Finally, the parents of these children had had enough. They sued the school board. The basic question the court had to decide was whether or not racial segregation was constitutional. The case was so important that it was heard by the Supreme Court of the United States. Thurgood Marshall knew he would have to use every bit of skill he had to win the case. When it was all over, Thurgood

Marshall and the NAACP had scored a big victory. The justices decided unanimously that segregation in schools was unconstitutional.

Thurgood Marshall later became the first African American judge on the Supreme Court. During his long career, he never paused in his battle for civil rights. And through his tireless efforts, he truly did help change the nation.

George Hayes, Thurgood Marshall, and James Nabrit leave the Supreme Court after winning the Brown *case.*

Rich Resources and Good Neighbors

Maryland may be a small state, but it has the fifth highest per capita income in the country. This high ranking is due largely to the thriving area called the Baltimore-Washington corridor. This area includes Baltimore, Washington, D.C., and the nearly forty-mile stretch in between. Almost ninety percent of Maryland's population lives in the Baltimore-Washington corridor, which has become the nation's fourth largest metropolitan area. Thousands of workers commute between these two cities and their suburbs every day. There is no doubt that Maryland's generous donation of land for our nation's capital in 1791 is still paying off today.

This area's contribution to Maryland's economy is in service industry employment. Service industry jobs are those that serve people rather than make a product. Taken as a whole, Maryland's service industries account for more than eighty percent of its gross state product, which is the value of all the goods and services it produces.

These technicians work at NASA's Goddard Space Flight Center. Government services are Maryland's second most important service industry.

The Metro train system carries thousands of workers each day between Washington, D.C., and Maryland's suburbs.

One reason for the large number of service industry jobs in the Baltimore-Washington corridor is that many government offices are located around the nation's capital. Many Maryland residents work for government agencies, such as the Bureau of the Census or the Social Security Administration. They also work in other government institutions, such as public schools, hospitals, and military bases. Other important service industries in the area are retail trade, including restaurants and stores, and wholesale trade, much of which is centered around the thriving port of Baltimore. Private health care, insurance, banking, and real estate are also crucial to Maryland's service economy.

Industries that use computers and other high-technology machinery are another specialty of the Baltimore-Washington corridor. In fact, more scientists and engineers in the corridor work in "high-tech" jobs than in any other metropolitan area in the United States. Over 3,500 high-tech facilities operate in the corridor, and the number continues to grow. In addition, some of the nation's top research facilities, such as the National Institutes of Health and the NASA-Goddard Space Flight Center, promise to keep Maryland on top as the nation's industries become increasingly technical.

The Baltimore-Washington corridor is also home to most of Maryland's manufacturing industry. Since World War II, manufacturing has declined in importance, but it still produces about $12 billion a year for the state's economy.

Electrical goods, especially computers and communications products, dominate Maryland's manufacturing industry. Food processing follows in importance. Many of the state's food-processing plants are in Baltimore, but other areas also benefit from this industry. For example, spices are produced north of Baltimore in Cockeysville, and seafood is packaged in Cambridge, on the eastern shore of the Chesapeake

This ship is being unloaded at the port of Baltimore. Transportation is one of Maryland's most important industries.

Maryland workers rake beans to be cooked and canned.

Tomatoes are unloaded at one of Maryland's food-processing centers.

Bay. Baltimore factories produce paint, household cleaners, and other chemical products. Chemicals are Maryland's third-ranked manufacturing industry.

Maryland isn't border-to-border factories and office buildings, however. About forty percent of the state's land is forest, and about 33 percent more is farmland.

Agriculture accounts for about one percent of Maryland's gross state product. Maryland's chief farm products are livestock, especially young chickens called broiler chickens. In fact, nearly half of the state's agricultural income comes from broiler chickens. Livestock farmers, mostly those in the western part of the state, also raise dairy cattle. Milk is Maryland's second most important farm product.

Among Maryland's important crops are corn, soybeans, and tobacco. Other agricultural products include decorative trees, flowers, and shrubs. Smaller vegetable and fruit farms produce tomatoes, apples, strawberries, and cucumbers.

Most of Maryland's coal resources are in the western part of the state.

Mining is another industry that accounts for a small percentage of Maryland's gross state product, yet it is important to its total economy. Crushed stone is the state's most valuable mining product, and coal is almost equally important. Although Maryland has never been noted nationally for its marble mining, quarry owners in Cockeysville are proud of their marble resources. In fact, the famous Washington Monument in the nation's capital holds some Cockeysville marble.

Seafood is one natural resource for which this coastal state is nationally known. Maryland is one of the leading states in the harvesting of crabs and oysters. Other key catches include flounder, clams, bass, and bluefish. Almost fifty million dollars' worth of seafood is hauled in from the Chesapeake Bay and the Atlantic Coast each year.

Maryland is also a popular vacation state. Baltimore alone draws more than five million visitors every year. Maryland also has many popular shoreline resorts. The Chesapeake Bay has the largest resort area on the East Coast, with over three thousand miles of beach. The resort town of Ocean City, which borders the Atlantic Ocean in the eastern part of the state, has a summer population that is many times larger than its year-round population.

Almost a third of the United States population and its industries are within a day's drive of Maryland. The ports along the Chesapeake Bay attract trade from around the world. And who could ask for a better economic neighbor than the nation's capital? With so many helpful neighbors enhancing the resources within its borders, Maryland's economy is in exceptionally good shape, now and for the future.

When these chicks are between five and twelve weeks old, they will be considered broiler chickens, one of Maryland's most important agricultural products.

This photo shows an oyster from the Chesapeake Bay. The oyster catch in the Bay has been significantly reduced in the past few decades because of pollution.

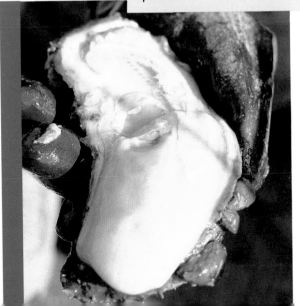

Smith Island

When Captain John Smith of Virginia first explored the Chesapeake Bay in 1608, he landed on a small island near the mouth of the bay. He named this "wondrous faire and delightsome" island after himself. But he never returned.

The history of Smith Island between then and now is sketchy. Some say British pirates who attacked American trade ships were the main inhabitants for much of its history. Most islanders deny that pirates were their ancestors, even though Rhodes Point, one of the island's three towns, was once called Rogues' Point. Whatever their histories, however, most of the five hundred or so people on Smith Island today lead very similar—and honest—lives, struggling to make a living from the Chesapeake Bay.

The community on Smith Island is very close-knit. There are no movies, no hospitals, no bars, no police, no jails, and no official government. The people who live here don't seem to need any of these things. The one thing that they do need, however, is the sea.

During peak season, a Smith Island soft-shell crab fisher rises before four in the morning and works well into the evening. Most crab fishers catch four to five hundred crabs a day. After expenses, all that a full day's work earns is about one hundred dollars. But ask Smith Island's residents if they'd like to make a better living, and most of them will say they're doing just fine.

Unfortunately, this peaceful way of life on Smith Island is endangered. Chemicals are polluting the Chesapeake Bay. Crabs are still thriving, but other types of seafood are disappearing. Seafood prices are going down, so few fishers can make a profit on their own. Some of the islanders are

Another day ends on Smith Island.

Blue-claw crabs are the most common type of crab sold as food in the United States.

looking to outsiders to make their living.

One of the islanders runs a boat that brings in about five thousand people a year. While many of these visitors stay only for a day, they spread the word about this secluded vacation spot. As a result, tourism is on the rise on Smith Island. Outsiders are planning to build hotels, marinas, and even an airport on the island. About a quarter of the island's houses are now owned by off-islanders. Since the fishing industry is shrinking, many young people have left the island to find jobs on the mainland. This means that the average age of the on-island population keeps getting older.

It's not that Smith Islanders are selfish. They're proud of their island and want to share it with people. But Smith Islanders are not prepared to make room for people who may not appreciate their island and their way of life. As fisher Jennings Evans said, "The water business is getting harder every day and I am just getting to feel like we're going against the grain of things. If we lost the water business, though, we'd lose our natural being." Perhaps Smith Island is just too beautiful to keep people away forever. One thing is certain, though. Its residents are going to hold on to their unique way of life for as long as they can.

A Sense of Community

Maryland's Prince George's County is home to many professional people. It is one of the largest suburbs of Washington, D.C. Over half its residents are African American. The 370,000 African Americans living in the suburb are among the best-educated and the wealthiest African Americans in the nation.

African Americans who tried to move to Prince George's County in the 1960s suffered from racial discrimination. Many people in the county were unfriendly to the newcomers simply because of their race. Even worse, the county government fought against laws that made it illegal to keep people out of certain neighborhoods because of their race. Many newcomers who did manage to find housing in the county lived in fear of racial violence.

All of these factors kept many African Americans from moving to Prince George's County at first. In 1970 less than 15 percent of the county's residents were African Americans.

But that 15 percent stayed on, giving courage to others who wanted to move to the suburb.

The business community of Prince George's County has also become increasingly African American. Today, many of the county's businesses are owned by African Americans.

Many residents of Prince George's County say they are not interested in creating an African American community. They simply want to raise their children among successful African

Easy access to Washington, D.C., is one of the benefits of living in Prince George's County.

Housing in Prince George's County is still very affordable.

This photo shows St. Thomas's Church in Prince George's County. Churches are an important force in the county's community development.

Americans. They feel their children will benefit from exposure to more positive African American role models living within the community. Bonnie Johns has lived in Prince George's County for over thirty years. She has helped the community through its transitions, especially with her work on the county school board. "I care about the individuals I know," she says, "and I care about what happens to children. And I guess that's what it's about. It's about people struggling to put the pieces together for each other, and I can't think of any place it's been done better than here in this county and in this state."

Monumentally Maryland

Baltimore has been known as the "Monumental City." Baltimore earned this nickname in 1829, when it hired a sculptor to create a historical monument. The result was Baltimore's own Washington Monument, a column statue of George Washington.

The word *monumental* has also come to mean "outstanding" or "very great." The arts have always been of monumental importance to Baltimore. The city has the nation's oldest music school, the Peabody Conservatory, which was established in 1868. The Peale Museum, founded in 1814, is one of the oldest art museums in the nation. Baltimore also supports its own symphony orchestra and opera company. It makes sense, then, that a city with such a monumental artistic presence has fostered artists who have made monumental contributions to American society.

Writer H. L. Mencken was one such artist. Mencken became famous for his columns in the *Baltimore Sun*, which he joined as Sunday editor in 1906. He was known for his quick mind and acid

Years ago, 45 lighthouses directed ships through Chesapeake Bay. This lighthouse has been restored and is now at the Calvert Marine Museum in Solomons.

tongue. Mencken was the editor of a literary magazine called the *Smart Set* in 1914, in which he wrote about two thousand book reviews. In 1923 he started another magazine, *American Mercury*. In this publication, he commented, often humorously, on society, politics, and American lifestyle. Mencken also authored a study of the modern American language. His wit and intelligence made him not only nationally famous, but world famous as well.

Upton Sinclair was another Baltimore writer who made a monumental literary contribution. Sinclair belonged to a class of writers called *muckrakers*. These writers focused on exposing corruption and poor social conditions in America. In his 1906 book, *The Jungle*, Sinclair wrote about the dangerous and unsanitary working conditions in Chicago's meat-packing plants. The power of his words led to government inspections and reforms that are still in effect today.

Adrienne Rich is a Baltimore poet and essayist who has made a monumental contribution to the women's rights movement. She also writes about problems she sees in America's society and government. Rich first gained widespread attention when she won the 1974 National Book Award for her collection of poems, *Diving into the Wreck*.

Although Rachel Carson was originally from Pennsylvania, she attended school at Johns Hopkins University in Baltimore. She spent the later part of her life in a town called Silver Spring, just outside Washington, D.C. A biologist with a keen eye, Carson startled the world with her monumental book *Silent Spring*. Published in 1962, this book warned that we

Rachel Carson's most famous book is *Silent Spring*. Carson also won the National Book Award in 1951 for *The Sea Around Us*.

were destroying the earth and ourselves through the careless use of pesticides. Many generations of environmentalists have been spurred to action by Carson's groundbreaking work.

Baltimore's monumental artists aren't all writers, however. Many consider "Lady Day," the great Billie Holiday, to be the best jazz vocalist of all time. Holiday made her debut at age 16 and was nationally renowned by the time she was 20. Billie Holiday never received any formal training, but no one ever thought she needed it! Her autobiography, *Lady Sings the Blues*, was later made into a movie.

Monumental is a word many people would use to describe Frederick Douglass's life. Douglass was not a cultural figure from Baltimore, but he greatly affected the culture of Maryland and the entire United States. Born a slave in Tuckahoe, Maryland, in 1817, Frederick Douglass learned to read at age eight. He had to learn in secret, because it was illegal in Maryland at the time to educate slaves. He escaped to the North in his early twenties and soon began to give speeches against slavery. Douglass wrote many powerful essays. His autobiography, *Narrative of the Life of Frederick Douglass*, was first published in 1845. It inspired countless Americans of all races to stand up for causes they believed in.

Maryland's culture isn't entirely reflected by its famous figures, though. For instance, sports play an important part in the state's culture, especially sports that involve horses. The Preakness Stakes, one of the three biggest horse races in the nation, is a yearly Baltimore event. The Maryland Hunt Cup, first held

Billie Holiday was possibly the greatest jazz vocalist of all time.

Born a slave in Tuckahoe, Frederick Douglass went on to become one of President Lincoln's advisors and a civil rights activist.

Maryland's monument to George Washington is a 178-foot column made of white marble.

below. More than 3.5 million people watched the Orioles play at Oriole Park at Camden Yards in 1992, the year it opened.

bottom. The wild ponies at Assateague Island State Park are descended from horses that were turned out to graze on the island in the seventeenth century.

in 1894, was the first American steeplechase. In this type of race, horses jump over various obstacles, such as hedges and walls. Maryland's state sport involves horses, too. Since 1842 Maryland has hosted annual jousting tournaments. Jousting today is different from the jousting during the Middle Ages. Today, contestants spear iron rings with their lances instead of other riders. It's not life or

St. Mary's County has many historical buildings such as the Sotterly Plantation.

death, but excitement still runs through the crowd when tournaments are held every October.

Historical monuments are preserved as artifacts and reminders in various places throughout the state. For instance, Baltimore's Maryland Historical Society holds the original manuscript of the "Star-Spangled Banner." In the southern part of the state, visitors can stroll through parts of St. Mary's City, Maryland's first settlement. It's been restored to appear as it did in the seventeenth century. The city even has a replica of the *Dove*, the ship that brought the city's first settlers from England. A more somber history can be revisited at Antietam National Battlefield in Sharpsburg, where Civil War soldiers fought one of the bloodiest one-day battles of the Civil War.

Many of Maryland's cultural landmarks and contributions reflect its heritage. By showing the state as it was in another time, we can judge the progress we've made—and how much we need to regain.

From the Jockey Club to the Preakness

You may have heard of or seen a Tennessee walking horse or a Kentucky thoroughbred. Maryland probably doesn't come to mind at all when you think of raising horses—but it should. In fact, central Maryland's concentration of thoroughbreds per square mile is twice that of Kentucky's.

The quality of Maryland-raised horses is increasing with the quantity. Take it from breeder and trainer Billy Boniface, who has made his Bonita farm one of the most successful horse farms in the state. Billy is convinced he's in the right place for raising winners. That's because Maryland's soil is good for growing bluegrass, which is highly nutritious for horses. "If I had to pick a place to raise a horse, I'd raise him right here in Maryland," says Billy. "Horses thrive in the spring in Maryland."

Horses are a billion-dollar industry in Maryland, perhaps because the state has had over 250 years to develop it. The Maryland Jockey Club was

The Preakness was named after the first horse to win a race at Pimlico.

founded in 1743, over thirty years before the Revolutionary War. George Washington frequently attended the club's races in the 1760s and 1770s. Andrew Jackson became a club member in the 1830s, while he was President of the United States.

Today, Maryland's biggest racing event is the Preakness Stakes, which was first run almost 125 years ago. Baltimore's Pimlico Race Course, the site of the Preakness, is the second oldest racetrack in the nation. This track dates back to 1870. The Preakness is one of the three classic horse races that make up the Triple

Central Maryland has many horse farms.

Crown. The other two are the Kentucky Derby and the Belmont Stakes. The Triple Crown is the most sought-after horse racing prize in the nation. Baltimore hosts a nine-day celebration before the Preakness at the end of May. The city launches hot-air balloons and fireworks and hosts festivals and a parade.

With so much history behind them and excitement surrounding them, how could Maryland's horses not grow up to be winners? And Billy Boniface thinks they're only going to get better. "For centuries we've been inbreeding them," he says. "We've made their bones finer. We've been putting more weight on their backs. We've been running them over harder racetracks, and yet they continue to break records year after year. They do the impossible every day!" If Maryland trainers like Billy Boniface keep up their dedicated work, maybe the state will soon give its name to a new breed of champions.

The rules of racing do not allow horses to race until they are two years old. Most horses that race are between two and five years old.

A Small State in the Big Leagues

Over the years, Maryland has proved itself well equipped to take on the future. Baltimore, Maryland's largest city, is a fine example. Like other cities around the country, Baltimore suffered when many of its residents moved to the suburbs. Its downtown area was all but abandoned as people moved their families—and their tax money—to new suburban neighborhoods. But the people remaining in Baltimore didn't panic. Instead they took their courage and intelligence in hand. They rebuilt their city, preserving its old neighborhoods while rebuilding a thriving downtown.

Baltimore hasn't stopped yet. A new international marine research and exhibition center is opening. A second international project in the works is the International Life Sciences Trade and Conference Center.

Other areas of the state have proved ready for the future, too. Towns within the Baltimore-Washington corridor, where space research and high technology point the way to the future, are a good example. The

Almost three thousand different kinds of animals and plants live in Chesapeake Bay and the nearby wetlands.

state is always preparing its next generation. In fact, Maryland has the nation's fourth highest percentage of residents with at least four years of college.

But such a positive outlook doesn't mean that Maryland has no room for improvement. Like many states, Maryland must keep an eye on the environment to ensure health for the future. But once again, Maryland is one step ahead of the game. The state began a Chesapeake Bay cleanup project in the mid-1980s, which is slated to continue into the next century.

Maryland accomplishes so much that people often forget that it's such a small state. As long as Maryland continues to put intelligence and foresight to good use, it will undoubtedly remain one of the big-league players in the nation's future.

The NASA/Goddard Space Flight Center at Greenbelt is the nation's main facility for tracking space vehicles.

Important Historical Events

1608 Captain John Smith sails from Virginia up the Chesapeake Bay and explores the Maryland region.

1631 William Claiborne sets up a trading post on Kent Island. It is the first European settlement in the Maryland area.

1632 The Maryland charter is given by King Charles I to Cecilius Calvert, the second Lord Baltimore.

1634 Leonard Calvert founds St. Mary's City.

1652 The Susquehannock, the last of the state's raiding Native Americans, turn over their land to the colonists.

1699 Maryland's first libraries are established by Dr. Thomas Bray.

1729 The city of Baltimore is founded.

1767 The Mason-Dixon Line is completed, establishing the boundary between Maryland and Pennsylvania.

1776 Maryland delegates vote for independence from Great Britain. Maryland adopts its first constitution.

1783 Annapolis becomes the temporary capital of the United States.

1784 The Treaty of Paris is signed at the Maryland State House in Annapolis, officially ending the Revolutionary War.

1788 Maryland becomes the seventh state of the Union.

1791 Maryland gives land to Congress for the District of Columbia, the nation's new capital.

1814 The British attack Fort McHenry in Baltimore during the War of 1812. The battle inspires Francis Scott Key to write "The Star-Spangled Banner."

1818 The National Pike is completed from Cumberland, Maryland, to Wheeling, Virginia.

1828 Construction begins on the Baltimore & Ohio Railroad.

1830 Peter Cooper runs the first American steam locomotive, *Tom Thumb*, out of Baltimore.

1837 The *Baltimore Sun* newspaper is first published.

1861 Although a slave state, Maryland decides to remain a part of the Union during the Civil War.

1862 The Union Army stops Confederate General Robert E. Lee in the Battle of Antietam, near Sharpsburg. Lee retreats to Virginia.

1867 Maryland adopts its current constitution.

1886 Construction of the Enoch Pratt Free Library begins in Baltimore.

1938 Maryland passes the nation's first state income tax law.

1942 Camp David opens.

1952 The Chesapeake Bay Bridge opens.

1967 Maryland is the first southern state to pass equal housing laws.

1972 Maryland establishes a state lottery.

1985 Maryland begins an environmental program to clean up Chesapeake Bay.

1994 Annapolis celebrates its three-hundred-year anniversary as the capital of Maryland.

Maryland's bright state flag was adopted in 1904. The red and white design is the coat of arms of the Crossland family, the first Lord Baltimore's relatives on his mother's side. The black and gold design is the coat of arms for the Calvert family, Lord Baltimore's relatives on his father's side.

Maryland Almanac

Nickname. The Old Line State

Capital. Annapolis

State Bird. Baltimore oriole

State Flower. Black-eyed Susan

State Tree. White oak

State Motto. *Fatti Maschii, Parole Femine* (Manly Deeds, Womanly Words)

State Song. "Maryland, My Maryland"

State Abbreviations. Md. (traditional); MD (postal)

Statehood. April 28, 1788, the 7th state

Government. Congress: U.S. senators, 2; U.S. representatives, 8. State Legislature: senators, 47; representatives, 141. Counties: 23, plus Baltimore, an independent city

Area. 10,455 sq mi (27,077 sq km), 42nd in size among the states

Greatest Distances. north/south, 124 mi (199 km); east/west, 238 mi (383 km). Coastline: 31 mi (50 km)

Elevation. Highest: Backbone Mountain, 3,360 ft (1,024 m). Lowest: sea level, along the Atlantic Ocean

Population. 1990 Census: 4,798,622 (14% increase over 1980), 19th among the states. Density: 459 persons per sq mi (177 persons per sq km). Distribution: 81% urban, 19% rural. 1980 Census: 4,216,941

Economy. *Agriculture:* broilers (young chickens), milk, nursery and greenhouse products, corn, soybeans, tobacco, tomatoes. *Fishing:* crabs, oysters, clams, many types of fish. *Manufacturing:* electrical equipment, food products, chemical products, printed materials. *Mining:* crushed stone, coal, sand, gravel

State Seal

State Flower: Black-eyed Susan

State Bird: Baltimore oriole

Annual Events

★ Children's Fair in Timonium (April)

★ Preakness Celebration in Baltimore (May)

★ National Pike Festival in Garrett and Washington counties (May)

★ American Indian Inter-Tribal Cultural Organization Pow Wow in McHenry (July)

★ Sailing Regatta in Rock Hall (July)

★ Calvert County Jousting Tournament in Port Republic (August)

★ State Fair in Timonium (August/September)

★ Renaissance Festival in Crownsville (August/October)

★ National Hard Crab Derby and Fair in Crisfield (Labor Day weekend)

★ Grand Militia Muster in St. Mary's City (October)

Places to Visit

★ Antietam National Battlefield, near Sharpsburg

★ B & O Railroad Museum in Baltimore

★ Babe Ruth Birthplace and Baseball Center in Baltimore

★ Banneker-Douglass Museum of African American Life and History in Annapolis

★ Fort McHenry National Monument and Historic Shrine in Baltimore

★ Historic St. Mary's City, near Lexington Park

★ Maryland Science Center and National Aquarium in Baltimore

★ NASA/Goddard Visitor Center and Museum in Greenbelt

★ Ocean City and Assateague Island